# and yet i feel

fragile heart

## celia sinclair
## e.m. handly

Two Ten Press

E.M. Handly
writing as
Celia Sinclair

Two Ten Press
twotenpress@gmail.com

eBook ISBN: 978-1-7367415-9-7
Print ISBN: 979-8-9887211-0-9

www.celiasinclair.net
www.emhandly.com

*To those who have taken a piece of my heart –*
*I am whole again.*

# contents

*my soul aches for closure*
*begs for forgiveness*
*hopes to heal*

*I am broken*
*and yet*
*I feel*

# wilted

am I destined to live
this life alone

conquering the heart
wrenching obstacles

carrying the full weight
of depraved dilemmas
life so graciously offers
in abundance

is it better for me this way

am I not in control
of all that surrounds me

maybe it is through
no fault
other than my own
that I am here

*- fated*

*you're so infantile!*

one day you shall see
the insignificance of
your petty grievances

may you wake
with a fearful twinge
in your stomach

all you have done
all you have said
no matter how righteous
you think you are

no matter how much
you hurt me

may you realize
you twisted the knife
further into
your own heart

*- baby daddy*

I should have
trusted you
the first time
saved some pain

you never lied to me
always given pure
unadulterated honesty

without regret
no shame

as I push your words
to the back of my mind
I tell myself be noble
give the benefit
of the doubt

once again
I feel the need
to tell myself
I told you so

*- instinct*

I can't sleep

visions of what used to be
haunt me as I chase
memories

a vicious reminder
of a heart
once so happy

after everything
I still love you
as if you never left

*- brian*

there has been this
intense longing
for some time now

maybe I think it could heal
the gaping wound
inside my chest

just to hold someone
again

see their face light up
with no long term
necessity

I miss the feeling
of something new

god...

I miss the feeling
of something old

*- familiar*

how many times
have I loved
and of these
was the love returned

should I question
the voice inside my head
or allow thoughts of you
to churn

one begs me to wait
says you'll soon change
your mind

the other says
*do it*
regret you'll find

how many times
have I loved
and of these
was the love returned

soul mates
truth and love
the concept
soon shall burn

- *grandiose*

thirty years later
he looks up and tells her
*ya know,*
*you just keep getting better*

to still see someone like that
to see them –
at all

after all the heartache
to this day
it's still
what I strive for

*- jealous*

oh the loathing
the self-pity
you poor
pathetic soul

*are you not the master*
*of your domain*

how long will you
blame others
for your insignificance

*- self*

the grass is always greener

'cause there is more shit
to fertilize it –
cousin told me that

you're doin' fine

having a weak moment
had to call someone

yeah, I'm alone

and you don't have
to take any shit

which is better?

neither.

*- bestie*

wishing you and your whore
the best on your engagement

in your years together
or lack thereof
may you cry many tears
your hearts forever hurt

and may you live
the very hell
that you have unleashed
into the lives of others

*- jaded*

and yet I feel

for too long
I have fought
this battle

setting sail
on a journey to
a distant island
all needs fulfilled

only to realize
I need more

*- unsatisfied*

I'm becoming bitter – untrusting
slowly making myself believe
no one will ever be worthy
of me

I am too good
for the bad boys
and too bad
for the good ones

who would have thought
men would rather
be with someone
no one else
would want

*- plain jane*

feelings surface
*why after all this time*

they were there before
and they were strong

they enter my dreams
but are they real

or could they be
visions of my past
enticement
temptation

*it feels right*

is there really such a thing
as my classification

some would wish to argue
deny *my* feelings
are true

*you're confused*
*you're hurt*
*you're manipulated*
they say

more importantly
am I willing to accept it
and voice the same

- *fiona*

new feelings have emerged
for someone I never expected
to be more than a friend

am I willing to accept
the repercussions
of all that comes
with her

disgusted looks
stares that last too long
not being treated the same
as *normal* couples

this isn't my first rodeo
two attractive women
unashamed in everything
that we are
together

                                        - *bisexual*

you were the first
in a long time

to absorb my words

feel them
analyze them

everything I attempt
to convey

9 times out of 10
understand them

you help me
to take a step back

allow my voice
to return

*- her*

you came back
as if you wanted
to actually try

given more of an effort
than the entire time
you had me completely

I can't help but feel
the need to conform
to another identity
so far removed
from my own

but you're communicating
so I have to make an attempt
no matter how small

either road I choose
everyone gets hurt

*- mike*

what the *hell* happened

my world is suddenly
spinning out of control
once again

so many thoughts
my mind is trying
to organize

feelings attempting
to find their place
in my heart

she is reminding me
to love myself

remember
who I want to be

*- unsure*

and yet I feel

—♡—

did I stir something
from within you

did you really have
an epiphany

do I finally have
your *attention*

                            *- awake*

love lost
never to be found

*is it in limbo*

quietly waiting

wanting so bad
to be noticed
to be embraced

never really lost

sitting on the back burner
waiting for the friction
to ignite the spark

I want to believe

however – I hesitate

I've given so much
never received in return

beneath and beyond
all the pain
you remain

and yet I feel

how can I not
give you the chance
no one else has taken

*- second time*

for memories linger
we shall never fade

my heart hurts
for I have hurt you

no longer concern
myself with the pain
I thought I felt

it was a mere attempt
to numb the feeling

*- unintentional*

back to negative thoughts

I understand
you have feelings
and a right to them
as I do mine

we made the decision
collectively
to try again

I refuse to have *anything*
thrown at my face

she is still
and will remain
my friend

*- reexamining*

I dream daily
to create new ways
of bringing back
your interest

time is my foe
distance an annoyance
*is there anything*
*in my favor*

I used to look at you
and you would return
that sexy grin

the one that told me
how bad you wanted
to touch me
kiss me

it's been a while

what I wouldn't give
to see it every day
for the rest of my life

*- yearning*

and yet I feel

I fear your silence

it screams to me
like rantings of
a homeless man
inconsistent – lonely

ready to rip
from the heart
the last hope of
anything sacred

throwing bits and pieces
into the city streets
to stick to the shoes
of passers by

*- communication*

I talk to the brick wall
inside your head
as my wishes for affection
continue to grow
with every word

my arms ache
for an embrace
my mind prays
for content

the winds continue
in the wrong direction
never blowing towards
my advantage

*- mistake*

I am not invisible

it appears you see me
sometimes

I know this because
sometimes
you speak to me

other times I might as well
be a fly on the wall

or rather toilet paper
unwillingly stuck
to the bottom of your shoe

I never signed up for
a weekend romance

never wanted to be
the means to an end
nor a mere convenience

but here is tuesday
and as I wipe away the tears,
I wonder how to walk away

*- hurt*

anxiety is killing me
always hated confrontation

the thought of telling you
is breaking my heart

and I know I'm going
to break yours

the beatles lied
love is not enough

*- needs*

and yet I feel

he expels too much
energy from me
inadvertently – of course

can't concentrate
on the norm

I want my freedom

I can't do this anymore

I don't really care
what you have to say

you were supposed
to love me
defend my honor

and I don't believe
you ever will

another sheep
strolling with the flock
conforming to every one else's
ideas and perceptions

*- really done*

———♡———

Why do we love so quickly
only to have it ripped from our grasp
as soon as it's revealed?

———♡———

# blooming

I can already feel
the first brush
of your hand

the first taste
of your lips

knowing
validating
every thought
that led us here

- *stephen*

it's heart wrenching

I have not waited
for a man's phone call
in quite some time

check my horoscope
hoping it will reveal
a chain of events
I so desperately want
to unfold

it's hard not to obsess
wondering what I've done
or said to relieve him of the
want of further inquiry

silly me...
does desperation
permeate from my skin

*- anticipation*

I'm not used to
dating someone
on a normal level

the ride was cold today
but the coffee was sweet

he hugged me

rubbed my legs
on the way home

I wanted to kiss him

touch him with
no strings attached

I'm going to ask him
out for drinks on friday

I'm going to make him
kiss me

*- free bird*

you were right

when I walk into a room
men take a second glance

but I never thought
he would take an interest

it must be his eyes
that burn through my soul

pierce every thought process
your mind can conceive
on contact

by the way, fiona
I win
he didn't bring flowers

*- something new*

time to work
that second job

show some leg
flash that fake smile
and pray
I make a buck

my money is never
my own anyway

maybe he'll come in
make this whole evening
worth while

I try and imagine
what his hands feel like

I'm sure his body
is nice and tight

at least it appears to be
in his uniform

I wonder if he thinks
the same of me

celia sinclair & e.m. handly

what if he's disappointed
with my rough
and tainted skin

*- not confident*

I've felt your skin
against mine
but I have yet
to feel *you*

your eyes seem to have
emotions behind them
yet I doubt your intensions

*what rock was my logic*
*hiding under*

I've had fuck buddies before
but at least they enjoyed
my company

I'm too old
to fuck and feel
and be hurt

you don't want to know me
and you don't want me
to know you

maybe the travel
bottle of shampoo
for colored hair

celia sinclair & e.m. handly

and the mandarin scented
body wash in your shower
gave it away

- *no thanks*

———♡———

The truth can only hurt
if in the beginning
it was hidden.

———♡———

———♡———

floating on a raft
surrounded by sea

you surface from below
swim towards me

our bodies embrace
as silver ripples reflect
from your eyes

I am safe

a salt-stained kiss
before I wake

*- merman*

———♡———

I wish I could remember
what it's like to be loved

what I wouldn't give
to recall hands
splendidly exploring
every intricate part
of my being

another mind
picking and prodding
at every thought
that trickles down
my temple

another heart
directly beating
above my own
breath to breath
beat to beat

for now, my heart
is numb

someone put a curse on me
snuck a poison in wine

celia sinclair & e.m. handly

I wait patiently
for the anecdote

*- desire*

and yet I feel

insanity wages war
with the sane

fantasy and reality
play a tug of war

what once seemed real
now raises questions

has my mind simply
created all this drama

or have I simply
begun to see through

*- awakened*

everyone thinks
they know you

you like to drink
she's an alcoholic

you like – want – *need*
sex
she's a whore

everyone's a critic

they don't really
know you
never even
spoke to you

that doesn't stop them
from passing their
twisted perceptions

small town
even smaller minds

*- fuck off*

find another muse

I have enough hate
and anger to suffice it

written too much
about love
carrying false hope

as if I have a reason

what I used to have
I no longer possess

you are to blame
for taking the part of me
which was strongest

making it cower
fearful to resurface
above your destruction

slowly picking up
the shattered pieces
building a wall
along the way

thick leather skin
no longer smooth
inviting everyone
to touch it

in desperate need
of repair

*- damaged*

———♡———

demeaning comments fly
from the mouths of those
with too much time on their hands
and too few intelligible interests

afraid to peer inside themselves
and analyze what it is that
makes them feel so empowered
by conversing about that or who
they know nothing about

that mysterious person that makes
their existence more interesting
by creating elaborate, vicious tales
releasing them to whoever will listen
and more importantly
who will believe

from each person whence it came
growing more exaggerated
becoming a malicious cycle of false
information, hurting individuals
and destroying reputations
along with a certain innocence

*- rumors*

he told me
how liberating it was
to get revenge

*I believe it feels*
*better to walk way*
*brand the real asshole*
I reply

I don't think he quite
understood

I wish I could acquire
a disturbing madness
in my soul
at times

giving me the power
to make one cry in defeat
with my mere presence

*- manny*

I am to tread lightly
because I may get
what I wish for

such a significant number

I dream of it
and it comes to me
with significant events
on the same day
every time

what will it
bring to me
today

*- 13th*

friday and saturday
I watch for you

you show up
approach the bar
smile –
send tingling messages
in all the right places

it must be the dimple

sexy next to those
straight perfect whites

plump lips I want to feel
against mine

I wonder if I ever will
feel them

I wonder if you're puzzled
by these same thoughts
and will we ever be so inclined
to voice them

*- flicker*

I think I've met
a gentleman

it's been a long time

seek and ye shall find

or stop worrying so much
and it will happen

murphy's law

the more you want something
the further you push it
from your grasp

I have *mastered* this

something must be
seriously wrong

must stand guard

- *sus*

he holds something
screaming to me –
safety

my typical bad boy image
pulling me in
weakening
my entire soul

still trying to decide
if it's more frightening
than any previous encounter

I wonder if he has
a little dick

do I get all I want
mentally – emotionally
in exchange for…

please – not *that*

he held me tonight

biceps flexed on my neck
lips on my bare skin –
strength in his grasp…

and yet I feel

he thinks I'm funny

I wonder how he is
with kids

*- rob*

my bleeding kiss
haunt your dreams
as I drink with hunger

we are a vast
naked flame
flickering together
in a dark embrace

*- eternal*

can't believe
I'm doing this
again

diamond ring
big house

he loves me
*right*

negative thoughts
still fight
their way through

wait…

too good
to be true

the women's intuition
we're all taught about
but never learned
to trust

*- maybe*

how can we start a life together
when remnants of your previous
excursion plagues us

my confidence is waning

how can you take me
from all of this
as I struggle
to save myself

you're different

or is it *me*

you've got issues

it was too soon

I saw the signs

I chose to ignore them

                    *- never again*

amazing how the male heart
regurgitates its prey
like a snake choking
up a dead rat

lifeless because the reptile
played with it longer
than it should have

now numb to manipulation
like a child, realizing
he's been made a fool of

screaming
I don't wanna
play anymore

*- games*

you said you loved
everything about me
total package

then *bam!*
you require I conform
to your set of standards

no – more

*please tell me*
*I can do this*
*on my own*

damn you
for everything

*I believed you*

angry with myself
for not seeing through
the bullshit

you wanted to give me
and my son
your last name

celia sinclair & e.m. handly

you can't control me
or anything I am
anything I say
anything I do

you mother fucker
feed your shit
to someone else
hungry for your lies
willing to drown themselves
in your meaningless drivel

how you hated that
I stood up for myself

your silly insignificant
manipulations will not
affect me

I will never comply

*- nice try*

one couple above
another below

I hear a baby crying

can't figure out where
it's coming from

I imagine
the apartment upstairs

I can hear the footsteps
above my head

pacing back and forth
heavily as if
they're in the room
next to me

I should offer them coffee

I've been where they are

baby must be asleep now

*- single white female*

my heart still hurts

not sure I can do this
alone

I tell myself
*you got this*
*be strong*

depending on myself
is a new concept

invigorating
yet – intimidating

everyone says
give it time

but what the hell
does *that* mean

I still think about you

wonder if I can ever
trust another man
again

you tore down
all the walls
I painstakingly built

hand picking every piece
with every lie you told

you did everything right
said all the right things
used the kid – the dog

you had everything
so well planned
down to every detail

you didn't count on
one minor element

originally, independence
and intelligence
was a sexy virtue

celia sinclair & e.m. handly

but it was ultimately
our demise

I will never forget
the words you spoke
to me in front of the cop

*well, if you would have
just left when I **told** you to*

even the cop
was surprised

keep your stupid
fucking diamond

*- not ur girl*

I feel so alone

no man could ever
appreciate what I have
to give

people keep saying
it's not you

sure as hell
feels like it

tired of being
disappointed

must learn
to trust myself

do not confuse us

don't push me away

when will they realize that

*I* will be the norm

some day

*why so bitter*

this is affecting me
more than it should

I am self-reliant
don't need –
want anyone
in my life

yet I wonder
why not *me*

I no longer want
to feel this way

I used to believe
in beautiful things

how immature
my younger self
has been

thank you
for showing me
the error of my ways

*- men*

celia sinclair & e.m. handly

my mind drifts
as nina simone
sings to me

been so long
since I felt
a man's touch

a lioness waiting
to be unleashed

*have you returned*
or is it lack of sleep

I knew you were
lurking amidst

peering over the wall
I inadvertently built
around my being

*- muse*

reel me in
a little further

*is your line*
*long enough*

*do you think*
*I'll take the bait*

a lonely fish flailing
in the open sea

having fallen
too many times before
hook line and sinker

only to be thrown back
into the lonely abyss

- *marcus*

I want to escape with you

even if only for a night

cleanse your mind

rejuvenate your body

remember your soul

I have deceived myself.

All this time, incoherently,
picking weeds when initially –

I had seen daises.

So enthralled in finding
the one that best compliments
everything it represents.

How long must I search
through the fields?

When will I breathe in
that enticing scent?

How long must I wait
to hold my idea
of perfection?

*- bloom*

when the heart is true
there lies no question

when you see love
feel it and live it

how can one dismiss it
as if it never existed

and return to the very hell
that had led them there
to begin with

*- denial*

and yet I feel

I long for the first touch
of your hand
the taste of your lips
faint whispers on
the small of my neck

knowing – validating
every thought
every sentiment
that has led us here

*- possibility*

I tend to do better
with meaningless flings.
They hurt much less.

You started as that
but have somehow
walked your way
into my heart.

One voice says take it
with a grain of salt.
Another begs me
to trust you.

Heaven forbid,
I fall in love and
have my heart broken
yet again.

*- Corey*

# corey

the numbness has subsided
but my concentration suffers

emotions once forbidden
eagerly welcomed
without hesitation
debilitating rationalization

and so it begins
you're a part of me now

traveling a familiar highway
I reach the exit ramp
slow down
get ready to pay the toll

a voice screams to me
*are you sure*
*this is the way*

unaware of construction ahead
I comply to the voices

never really had
a great sense of direction

my foot hits the gas
hoping – praying
from here
I'll find my way home

*- lovers beware*

and yet I feel

if you could walk
through my thoughts
and dance with my heart
you would not be
so apprehensive

we are cosmically connected
not a mere coincidence

extracting small parts
to take with us
once we realize
the pain staking truth

*- coupled*

two people tired
of individual society
seemingly regurgitated

strangely creating a façade
of honesty – integrity
a sense of self

only to reveal
self-loathing and fighting
inner demons mysteriously
strange to us

should we be so inclined
to believe another force
has curiously introduced us

*- tired*

you're a bad drug
playing with my emotions

although I know
you're no good for me

the temptation is too strong
to deny

*- addiction*

celia sinclair & e.m. handly

———♡———

you are the eyes
I am the voice

two hearts – two minds
infinite possibilities

———♡———

god I love this man

it's so different
than any time before

he asks me how I know
but the words fail to form

I fear he thinks
I'm unsure

he loves everything
about me

tattoos on my skin
rebelliously short hair
anything I do that strays
from the norm

he doesn't complain
leaves it to me to decide
my own fate

he appreciates my art
and I his
he's so talented
able to see the beauty

in things most overlook

his fingers outline
every inch of me

fine details in my neck
from stern to stomach
like a boy seeing a female
naked for the first time

his perception amazes me
and reminds me of the beauty
I once saw myself

he is everything to me
best friend – lover

I trust him

I believe him

*- Us*

I hope you can handle me

all my little nuances

you worry I'll get bored
with you and yet
I fear the same

I can be overwhelming

over react in my insecurities
but everything fits together
so perfectly

I love your company

the way you express
everything on your mind

forgive me if I hesitate

every dream I've dreamt
every poem I've written

thinking you were
just a figment of
my imagination

afraid of going there alone

there's a sense of knowing
I cannot deny

when you clasp
my hand in yours
I have never felt
so wanted – so safe

*- real*

you come to me and open up
enough to make me wonder
and just as your about to speak
the thoughts
they crawl back under

there's so much that you want to say
so much you must release
yet fear and pride are keeping you
from bringing your mind to peace

don't assume you're a burden
by getting things off your chest
rather it should help you
put your worries to rest

one day I hope you come to know
the more you share your thoughts
the more our love
will grow

*- trust*

I knew coming into this
there would be sacrifices

I'm at a point in my life
there are things
I can live without
things I'd much rather have

another door has opened
even though I know not
what lurks on the other side

I'll walk through it
with the same excitement
fear and anticipation
as I have the others

reminding you along the way
I would give up my life
as I know it
to live with you
in yours

*- starting over*

I wish I could say to you
every word my pen writes

if you only knew all
that you have given

you couldn't possibly

as it is returned to you
therefore never missed

I wonder where time
will lead us

hearts linked
souls bound cosmically

endlessly seeking –
reaching – growing

will this love
become that of greatness

or does my mind deceive me

*- mind tricks*

slow, methodical movement
hearts racing – heating exteriors

the breath
the moans

lips together –
then apart

*is there music playing*

rhythm pounding each
raging part of our being

nothing left to do
but surrender

*- ecstasy*

all I want
all I ever want
is to love you

for as long as
time will allow

please don't be afraid

love does not hurt
it can only comfort

when the heart breaks
your mind thought
something was
that was not

when your heart sings
it knows of that
which really *is*

- *truth*

someone new
has entered my life
bringing with him
an aura of wonder
pleasure –
comfort

a part of me I thought
had run away
beside my broken heart

merely hiding with
the covers over her head
afraid to peek out

fearing the monsters
awaiting the opportunity
to viciously pummel her
back into seclusion

hoping –
wholeheartedly
to never again
be lost in the dark
and afraid

*- daybreak*

if you could crawl
inside me –
feel the electricity reverberate
through my bones

then maybe you would know

if you could walk along
my relentless mind
bear my thoughts
of the future

the maybe you would know

if you could hold my heart
in your hands – witness
how you have consumed it

then maybe you would know

*- not fleeting*

and yet I feel

—♡—

although she knew it was only temporary
she placed a band-aid on the gaping wound

—♡—

celia sinclair & e.m. handly

painfully pulling pins
and needles firmly
embedded over time

each bloodless extraction
providing certain
relief

the final one removed
from far beneath
the skin

fluids flow from the wound
offering a convoluted sense
of freedom

*- sovereignty*

I can see our future

a world of love – art
visual and literary

bringing optimism
and hope to this
miserable existence

encouraging each other
to continue to create –
breed all that is virtuous

we have so much
to offer individually
yet so much more
we can accomplish together

from every bad experience
I stole a small piece
to keep for myself

the only piece that kept me there
for any length of time

I would pocket it
file it away –

celia sinclair & e.m. handly

locked in my secret place
and wait

who knew – the heartbreak
to be endured

so much collateral damage
to achieve what so long ago
I deemed impossible

never knew the pain
would be so worth it

*- epitome*

my heart hurts

been watered down
and rung out

torn down
and taken apart

through all the abuse
once again able

to love again

I entered your dominion blindly
never knew what to expect.
Afraid of what might happen
from one day the next.

Negativity had bore a core
my heart had never felt.
All thoughts and dreams
consumed with the cards
that have been dealt.

Never in my wildest dreams
would I have pictured it this way.
Every night I close my eyes
looking forward to each new day.

Sometimes I have thoughts
this could all be wrong.
Again my eyes meet yours,
I am right where I belong!

*- pleasantly surprised*

so many thoughts
need to be expressed
my pen flounders
at where to begin

the more time
we spend together
all the more I want

each new thing
I learn about you
the deeper
I want to explore

something so new
so rich and primed –
leading myself to believe
it can remain so

will I be so blessed
to see it reach a plateau

*- something old*

celia sinclair & e.m. handly

— ♡ —

fear fails to escape me

too many times jumping in
being assured there are
no rocks at the bottom

the water feels good
exhilarating – refreshing

blindly leading me
to the coral reef to
slice through every
good intention

cutting through trust
scarring the heart

everything numb
from the pain

*- cautious*

my heart is resilient
my mind even stronger
yet they both must
be treated with kid gloves

not because I am feeble
or pathetic but because
I have a heart

that would be the
animate object beneath your chest
with which you feel
many emotions in concert
with your brain

I sometimes wonder
if yours work together

*- mean*

you love me
but you don't

when it all fits
your idealism
you're cool
happy – content

heaven forbid one
thing set you off
regardless if I
am responsible

I try to do right
by you but it's
never enough

*when is it going to be*

*- good enough*

—♡—

irrelevant
disheartening words
played across his lips
danced with his tongue

solace finding him
in his ignorantly
fueled rant

tears leapt from my lids
seeking solitude from the pain
as I took another sip
from my wine glass

*- drowning seclusion*

celia sinclair & e.m. handly

———♡———

*is this the life I longed for*

completely in love with a man
who seems to do nothing
but hurt me

it almost seems intentional

to feel you found your person

given your mind
body – soul

receive in return neglect
disrespect

continual reminders
nothing is good enough

no matter how hard you try
you still need to try harder

must I always be the one
to say I'm sorry

do I always have to beg
for your attention

and yet I feel

what happened to me
being the most important
person in the room

*- confused*

celia sinclair & e.m. handly

I am weak

though I long
for my alter-ego
to take control

she doesn't put up
with anyone's shit

she is strong
confident
unapologetic

I wish her tendencies
were more fluid
more predictable

why as the inevitable
shadows cast themselves
does she shrink

how does the result
of one word – one opinion
so drastically change
from one breath
to the next

and yet I feel

at this moment
it appears I care

tomorrow she won't

*- split*

celia sinclair & e.m. handly

you try
to do right

until you're unsure
of what that is

everything is enough
until it isn't

you flounder
question what is

answers make sense
until they don't

solutions simplified
until they aren't

I thought I was right
I thought I had the answers

- *wrong*

I haven't lost you completely
but the rain continues to fall

under an unsteady shelter
I wait for the storm to pass
so I can see the rainbow

follow it to my pot of gold

every storm passes in time
but is the damage done
worth salvaging

celia sinclair & e.m. handly

the waves crash the beach
completely resonating
with my emotions

the moon watches over me
as you fade into the trees

the crickets sing a song
of summers end

as I look out onto
the horizon and
wonder of great things
to come

positive energy swells
from within my heart
everything peaceful
once again

no idea where
we're supposed to go
as long as we go
together

*- moving forward*

never has one person
been able to make
my heart hurt so much

then fill the void
they created

my heart *feels* complete

one word – one swift action
it spirals down the rabbit hole
once so familiar

spinning uncontrollably
into infinite blackness

he is dark
he is light

I can't think of anything
more unfair

*- torn*

celia sinclair & e.m. handly

~♡~

we're broken

bringing each other
a sense of wholeness
belonging – acceptance
trust – loyalty

you are mine
and I am yours
free to be who
and what we are

wants – needs – desires
understood

if you only knew
how deep you burrowed
yourself within my soul

forever I give myself
to you

everything that I am
everything we can be
together

*- disasters*

and yet I feel

———❧———

my heart overwhelmed
with this feeling

afraid of drowning
in its own passion

there is nowhere to direct it
nothing to embrace it

damned to choke
from the abundance

———❧———

celia sinclair & e.m. handly

after everything endured
I believe you thought
I deserved to venture

it was me
who took the brunt of it
after all

I know you hurt as well
though you'll never admit it
never discuss it

we both lost something
that day

but I also know
we gained so much more

I received no sympathy from you
but I can't resent you for that

we deal with things
differently

placed in a situation
physically – mentally–
medically – unexpected

you never pretended
to understand

how could you
*possibly*

and you never made me feel
guilty for my decision

*- my body my choice*

I cried again last night
and a little more respect for him
trickled down my cheek

I grow tired
of playing the hard
ass bitch for you

I'm a woman
meant to be vulnerable
at times

it doesn't help
it *never* helps
when you say
*I don't give a shit*

you're cruel and cold
and all I want
is for you to acknowledge
your actions

I defend myself
and you're offended

*well, what makes you*
*so fucking special*

don't tell me to relax
don't tell me to lighten up

celia sinclair & e.m. handly

you don't have to feel
the way I do
about *anything*

just please give me
the same courtesy

*- hypocrite*

it's a love/hate relationship

cliché – maybe
truthful – for sure

we feel so much
yet allow idiosyncrasies
to rule us
guide us

I'm too serious
you're not serious
enough

I'm not spontaneous
you're too whimsical

what we once loved
about each other
has somehow
become a burden

there has to be
a happy medium

*- meet me in the middle*

celia sinclair & e.m. handly

many may not understand
everything I see as good

they don't need to

this is my own fault
they dislike him

when things aren't
loving and communicative
I feel the need to vent
to those closest to me

they only hear half
of the story

I can't allow
their negative thoughts
to form my opinions

what I know to be true
to my heart

it's not a romance novel

*- oversharing*

that fleeting moment
only lasts a second

but in that instant
you've fallen

and everything
is different

it's all so bitter-sweet
because you realize

you may just die
if he ever leaves

*- momentary lapse*

celia sinclair & e.m. handly

*continue the journey in What Forever
Feels Like*

For more information visit
www.emhandly.com
or www.celiasinclair.net